Contents

Legal 4

Why I wrote this book 5

Carrier Class VoIP Services 7

Building OS 9

    Basics 11

    INSTALL ALL SERVER TOOLS 12

    INSTALL HA package (High Availability) 13

    HeartBeat 14

    PaceMaker 15

        Install 17

        Create the Cluster 18

        Start the Cluster 19

        Set Cluster Options 20

        Add a Resource 21

        Simulate a Service Failure 22

    Setup HA 23

    Now What 25

MySQL 26

    Master / Master 27

        Step 1 - Install and Configure MySQL on Server A 28

        Step 2 - Install and Configure MySQL on Server B 31

        Step 3 - Completing Replication on Server A 34

        Step 4 - Testing Master-Master Replication 35

    Tables 37

    Create Database Tables 38

        Create table cdr 39

Create table extensions 41

Create table meetme 42

Create table queue_table 43

Create table queue_member_table 45

Create table sip_buddies 46

Create table voicemail_users 49

Now What 51

Asterisk 52

Features 54

Call Features 55

Privacy 57

Computer-Telephony Integration 58

Scalability 59

Speech 60

Codecs 61

VoIP Protocols 62

Traditional Telephony Protocols 63

ISDN Protocols 64

Installing 65

Special Configuration 68

cdr_mysql.conf 69

extconfig.conf 70

extensions.conf 71

modules.conf 72

res_config_mysql.conf 73

sip.Conf 74

RealTime 76

Three ways to access the data 77

In laymen's terms...78

Terminology/Files 79

How to configure RealTime - ODBC Method 80

How to configure RealTime - MySQL Method 81

Extconfig - Static Configs..82

Extconfig – RealTime...83

Now What...85

Interfaces GUI's..86

Legal

All Software and Operating systems are open source are readily available online along with the user agreements.

I make no assumptions that any information contained within this book is my original work or unique in any manner only that the configuration and combinations are unique.

This book is a reference to information available however the methods used within this book are the methods I have developed over many years of trial and error.

This book cannot be duplicated or copied in any manner without written approval of the author.

Asterisk is a trademark as well as Digium and I make no assumptions that either company endorses this publication.

Redhat, CentOs and Fedora EUA are available at their respected sites. I can't do all of the work for you.

Why I wrote this book

I have been working within the VoIP industry for over 18 years with the bulk of it being wrapped around Asterisk and other early open source projects. I have an extensive background in software development and all major programming languages on all major operating systems including early development of Communication Protocols, Telecom and TCP/IP protocols. I've said this so that you may have a little bit of a background on just who I am.

I've chosen to simply write and freelance VoIP support these days and I find myself in the same situations all the time. I usually get a call from someone who thinks that they have installed an Asterisk system and thinks that the quick easy way was the way to go and all should work fine. There are many issues with this line of thought and with the business model that was in place when they installed the system. Now I'm not saying that everyone that calls me are idiots, the bulk of them have made extremely stupid mistakes and I will explain why.

Biggest mistake that is made is they think like an end user and love windows, yes even the ones that run a flavor of Linux on their laptops love windows. How can I say that? Well it's easy they have installed a Linux system with a GUI (Graphical User Interface) to make it look and feel like a windows operating system so that they can easily find their way around. They then brag to their friends that they run Linux and think that makes them special. Fact is they are special but not in a good way.

End Users also like to think that it's ok to run several major services / systems on a single computer and that VoIP will play nice with it. Fact is if it wasn't for VoIP that train of thought might work and has with larger servers coming out every day with more and more memories that is becoming a standard.

End users love the windows feature of click to install, using an EXE or MSI. The make the assumption that all systems are the same. That's because they have usually either grown up in a world where end users are restricted to what they can do (Apple and IPhone) so as to protect the systems running the devices. Apple made a fortune treating end users as idiots and the yuppies enjoy being treated that way. They didn't care that they couldn't access any real system features or that any software written for the devices had to comply to Apple's idiotic standards.

In the following chapters we will address these issues and more as well as explain why this thinking was incorrect and how to do it correctly in the future, we will discuss all relative information from installation to final product of a carrier class system that can be maintained and trusted

Because this was originally formatted for eBooks there are references in here to click on for emailing and visiting mu other books so here is one that has the actual email.

If you find yourself wanting consulting or further information, then feel free to email me direct at AsteriskHA@3states.net any time and I will do my best to answer your questions ASAP

Carrier Class VoIP Services

Carrier class services requires an extremely high level of uptime and redundancy. It cannot be a service that has multiple points of failure and to achieve this we always should take certain steps to ensure there are minimal points of failure.

Certain functions are a must be included:

Uptime

Backup

Redundancy

Servers

Asterisk

Database

Administration

Power

CDR (Call Detail Records)

Legacy services and functions

Caller ID

Voice Mail

Call Waiting

Roll over

Auto Attendant

?

Some things to remember are that gamers are NOT by default computer nerds and to make Asterisk work as a carrier class service and administer it completely without help you must have to have certain knowledge in VoIP, Networking, Telecom, Programming (Multiple programming languages), OS's as well as dealing with end users. Anything short would make you not qualified to handle and efficiently troubleshoot issues that may arise.

VoIP has many components that all tie together to make the end user not aware of the fact their call is a typical VoIP call is using many different technologies all at one time. This should be accomplished by putting all the components together in a manner that is easy to administrate as well as having the fewest breaking points as possible.

Wikipedia's definition of Carrier Class is;

"In telecommunication, a "**carrier grade**" or "**carrier class**" refers to a system, or a hardware or software component that is extremely reliable, well tested and proven in its capabilities. Carrier grade systems are tested and engineered to meet or exceed "five nines" high availability standards, and provide very fast fault recovery through redundancy"

My last installation was for an internet service provider that wanted to become a VOIP provider as well. Setup was easy and now his clients are praising the quality of the service as well as the reliability of the service. This is because I put together a system that was quality and understand the inner workings of VOIP.

If you find yourself wanting consulting or further information, then feel free to email me direct at My Direct Email any time and I will do my best to answer your questions ASAP

Building OS

The OS is the core of any VoIP system and you must control every aspect of it. That is accomplished by first knowing the OS so pick a flavor of Linux that you are familiar with and by that I mean know your way around it without a GUI, if you aren't familiar with any then hire someone who is. I myself prefer a stable release of Fedora or Cent OS but any will work if properly setup and configured. I am not going to give step by step instructions on the installations because there are too many flavors to choose from and they change constantly.

People fail to realize that GUI's are just programs that make it so an idiot can get around the system with ease. Since it's a program or a group of programs it uses your resources, resources that you do want to use. GUI's like any other program can be a point of failure and we are minimizing all points of failure so DO NOT USE A GUI.

Install;

When installing most operating systems will give an option of what packages to choose from.

DO NOT CHOOSE ANY GUI'S

INSTALL ALL DEVELOPMENT PACKAGES

MYSQL and MYSQL-DEVEL

Standard hard drive partitions should be fine

Email server

Web server – we won't use it but we might use some of its features and packages

INSTALL ALL SERVER TOOLS

INSTALL HA package (High Availability)

INSTALL PaceMaker

INSTALL Heartbeat

Upgrade the OS

Something like "yum update"

Setup server

Make sure that you have correct network settings for connectivity

Test SSH connections

Connect from outside world.

Look at memory and usage

By using "top" you can see CPU and memory usage.

Make sure it doesn't have major usage. There should be barely any usage at this point.

If you want to install the basic Git tools on Linux via a binary installer, you can generally do so through the basic package-management tool that comes with your distribution. If you're on Fedora for example, you can use yum:

```
$ sudo yum install git-all
```

If you're on a Debian-based distribution like Ubuntu, try apt-get:

```
$ sudo apt-get install git-all
```

Basics

We won't go into too much detail on installation of the OS except to say that most installation CDs will give these basic options below. If you choose these then all will be will.

DO NOT CHOOSE ANY GUI'S OR DESKTOP ENVIROMENTS

INSTALL ALL DEVELOPMENT PACKAGES

MYSQL and MYSQL-DEVEL

Standard hard drive partitions should be fine

Email server

Web server – we won't use it but we might use some of its features and packages

INSTALL ALL SERVER TOOLS

We don't install GUI's because they just use resources that you do not need unless you're a moron gamer and as stated earlier, a gamer doesn't equal computer technician or intelligence as much as it does equal a total waste of time and resources.

We do install server and development tools. So in your guided installation process take care to select these.

INSTALL HA package (High Availability)

High availability is a characteristic of a system, which aims to ensure an agreed level of operational performance for a higher than normal period.

There are three principles of system design in high availability engineering:

1. Elimination of single points of failure. This means adding redundancy to the system so that failure of a component does not mean failure of the entire system. See Reliability Engineering.
2. Reliable crossover. In multithreaded systems, the crossover point itself tends to become a single point of failure. High availability engineering must provide for reliable crossover.
3. Detection of failures as they occur. If the two principles above are observed, then a user may never see a failure. But the maintenance activity must.

Modernization has resulted in an increased reliance on these systems. For example, telecom, hospitals and data centers require high availability of their systems to perform routine daily activities. Availability refers to the ability of the user community to obtain a service or good, access the system, whether to submit new work, update or alter existing work, or collect the results of previous work. If a user cannot access the system, it is - from the user's point of view - *unavailable*. Generally, the term *downtime* is used to refer to periods when a system is unavailable.

Most operating systems will permit you to install HA packages either during install or a basic yum install commands. Here is a simple guided list for installing.

HeartBeat

Heartbeat is a daemon that provides cluster infrastructure (communication and membership) services to its clients. This allows clients to know about the presence (or disappearance!) of peer processes on other machines and to easily exchange messages with them.

In order to be useful to users, the Heartbeat daemon needs to be combined with a cluster resource manager (CRM) which has the task of starting and stopping the services (IP addresses, web servers, etc.) that cluster will make highly available. Pacemaker is the preferred cluster resource manager for clusters based on Heartbeat.

Here is a basic list for installing Heartbeat in CentOS, change version info to match yours;

First begin to enabling EPEL repos

rpm -Uvh http://download.fedoraproject.org/pub/epel/6/x86_64/epel-release-6-8.noarch.rpm

While we don't use HearBeat directly and leave that to Pacemaker and even though PaceMaker installs the parts that it needs to run, it's always a good ideal to have complete packages installed for future development.

PaceMaker

In order to be useful to users, the Heartbeat daemon needs to be combined with a cluster resource manager (CRM) which has the task of starting and stopping the services (IP addresses, web servers, etc) that cluster will make highly available.

Heartbeat originally came with a primitive resource manager, however this is only capable of managing 2 nodes and could not detect resource-level failures.

A new resource manager which addressed these limitations and more was written for Heartbeat 2.0.0.

In 2007 the new resource manager was spun-off to become in order to better support additional cluster stacks (such as Corosync).

Information about Pacemaker is available from the project web site.

I will show you in this tutorial how to install your first cluster Corosync and the Linux Cluster Manager Pacemaker.

Let me give small definitions about Corosync and Pacemaker.

The **Corosync Cluster Engine** is an open source project licensed under the new BSD License derived from the OpenAIS project. The mission of the Corosync effort is to develop, release, and support a community-defined, open source cluster executive for use by multiple open source and commercial cluster projects or products.

Pacemaker is open source high availability resource manager software used on computer clusters since 2004. Until about 2007, it was part of the Linux-HA project, then was split out to be its own project.

From PaceMaker's directions;

All examples assume two nodes that are reachable by their short name and IP address:

node1 - 192.168.1.1

node2 - 192.168.1.2

The convention followed is that **[ALL] #** denotes a command that needs to be run on all cluster machines, and **[ONE] #** indicates a command that only needs to be run on one cluster host.

Install

Pacemaker ships as part of the Red Hat High Availability Add-on. The easiest way to try it out on RHEL is to install it from the Scientific Linux or CentOS repositories.

If you are already running CentOS or Scientific Linux, you can skip this step. Otherwise, to teach the machine where to find the CentOS packages, run:

[ALL] # cat < /etc/yum.repos.d/centos.repo [centos-7-base] name=CentOS-$releasever - Base mirrorlist=http://mirrorlist.centos.org/?release=$releasever&arch=$base arch&repo=os #baseurl=http://mirror.centos.org/centos/$releasever/os/$basearch/ enabled=1 EOF

Next we use yum to install pacemaker and some other necessary packages we will need:

[ALL] # yum install pacemaker pcs resource-agents

Create the Cluster

The supported stack on RHEL7 is based on Corosync 2, so thats what Pacemaker uses too.

First we set up the authentication needed for **pcs**.

[ALL] # echo CHANGEME | passwd --stdin hacluster [ONE] # pcs cluster auth node1 node2 -u hacluster -p CHANGEME --force

We now create a cluster and populate it with some nodes. Note that the name cannot exceed 15 characters (we'll use 'pacemaker1').

[ONE] # pcs cluster setup --force --name pacemaker1 node1 node2

Start the Cluster

[ONE] # pcs cluster start --all

If all goes right then you now have a cluster of servers running together, fairly cool and simple, don't you think?

Ok as a nerd I sometimes get caught up in the little things and like to ramble. I figure that if you're going to have OCD then put It to use.

Set Cluster Options

With so many devices and possible topologies, it is nearly impossible to include Fencing in a document like this. For now, we will disable it.

[ONE] # pcs property set stonith-enabled=false

One of the most common ways to deploy Pacemaker is in a 2-node configuration. However, quorum as a concept makes no sense in this scenario (because you only have it when more than half the nodes are available), so we'll disable it too.

[ONE] # pcs property set no-quorum-policy=ignore

For demonstration purposes, we will force the cluster to move services after a single failure:

[ONE] # pcs resource defaults migration-threshold=1

Add a Resource

Let's add a cluster service, we'll choose one doesn't require any configuration and works everywhere to make things easy. Here's the command:

[ONE] # pcs resource create my_first_svc Dummy op monitor interval=120s

"**my_first_svc**" is the name the service will be known as.

"**ocf:pacemaker:Dummy**" tells Pacemaker which script to use (Dummy - an agent that's useful as a template and for guides like this one), which namespace it is in (pacemaker) and what standard it conforms to (OCF).

"**op monitor interval=120s**" tells Pacemaker to check the health of this service every 2 minutes by calling the agent's **monitor** action.

You should now be able to see the service running using:

[ONE] # pcs status

or

[ONE] # crm_mon -1

Simulate a Service Failure

We can simulate an error by telling the service to stop directly (without telling the cluster):

[ONE] # crm_resource --resource my_first_svc --force-stop

If you now run **crm_mon** in interactive mode (the default), you should see (within the monitor interval of 2 minutes) the cluster notice that **my_first_svc** failed and move it to another node.

Setup HA

Here we will setup the part of HA that is important to us with Asterisk in use. That part is simply the virtual IP address. While HA has many other functions it's important that as a carrier class service that we only use resources that are needed and keep as few services running on the servers as possible.

For our configuration we only need;

pcs resource create OurVirtualIP ocf:heartbeat:IPaddr2\ip=(put virtual IP address here) cidr_netmask=32 op monitor interval=10s

Eliminate other resources that you may have created earlier;

Execute

pcs status

Cluster name: mycluster

Last updated: Thu Jan 7 13:36:46 2016   Last change: Mon Jan 4 23:22:31 2016 by root via cibadmin on pcmk-1

Stack: corosync

Current DC: pcmk-1 (version 1.1.13-10.el7-44eb2dd) - partition with quorum

2 nodes and 1 resource configured

Online: [pcmk-1 pcmk-2]

Full list of resources:

WhatevernameWeGaveIt (ocf::heartbeat:IPaddr2):   Started pcmk-1

PCSD Status:

  pcmk-1: Online

  pcmk-2: Online

Daemon Status:

  corosync: active/disabled

  pacemaker: active/disabled

  pcsd: active/enabled

under the section that gave "full list of resources:" remember the names that it list

remove all names but the one we named earlier "OurVirtualIP" by executing;

pcs resource delete (The other Names)

Run that command until you are only left with "OurVirtualIP".

You're ready to move on.

Now What

Pat yourself on the back you now have a real OS installed that isn't made for an idiot. It may very well be the first time ever you have been in front of such a powerful system. Many have tried most have failed doing this basic step.

I know it doesn't look like much, what with a black screen and a curser blinking to the right of a login prompt, but you have an operating system that is not made for games to be played on or for social media to be surfed. You know have an operating system that is completely ready for the business world and can handle task that most can only dream about.

Ok I get carried away a bit but you did well and now have a solid operating system to use in our next steps.

If you find yourself wanting consulting or further information, then feel free to email me direct at:AsteriskHA@3states.net any time and I will do my best to answer your questions ASAP

MySQL

Either one below is suitable as they are both the same for the most part.

MySQL is one of the most reliable and most recognized database systems out there as well as having most user friendly programming APIs available on the market.

MariaDB is a community-developed fork of the MySQL relational database management system intended to remain free under the GNU GPL. Being a fork of a leading open source software system, it is notable for being led by the original developers of MySQL, who forked it due to concerns over its acquisition by Oracle. Contributors are required to share their copyright with the MariaDB Foundation.

The think about MySQL is that not only is it open source but it is extremely stable as well as proven to operate under heavy usage without issues. MySQL is very close to MS-SQL without all of the fees associated with it. With the many tools available for development it will come in handy for us in the next book http://amzn.to/1negZhM and you can feel free to get on the mailing list for it here by

TechBook-mailinglist@3states.net.

A call-center that we designed used asterisk and the MySql database without issue. This system had well over a million queries a day and ran with little to no workload on the processor.

Master / Master

MySQL replication is the process by which a single data set, stored in a MySQL database, will be live-copied to a second server. This configuration, called "master-slave" replication, is a typical setup. Our setup will be better than that, because master-master replication allows data to be copied from either server to the other one. This subtle but important difference allows us to perform MySQL read or writes from either server.

This configuration adds redundancy and increases efficiency when dealing with accessing the data and is the primary reason for doing the setup this way however it is not the only reason. When we have other applications using the same database that is located on the primary server we are defeating the purpose of having a carrier class system (Remember we want as little to operate on the system as possible) so to keep this method up when we create an application we have it use the secondary database as well as publishing it on another server altogether.

Step 1 - Install and Configure MySQL on Server A

The first thing we need to do is to install the MySQL-server and MySQL-client packages on our server. We can do that by typing the following:

sudo apt-get install mysql-server mysql-client

By default, the MySQL process will only accept connections on localhost (127.0.0.1). To change this default behavior and change a few other settings necessary for replication to work properly, we need to edit /etc/mysql/my.cnf on Server A. There are four lines that we need to change, which are currently set to the following:

#server-id   = 1

#log_bin   = /var/log/mysql/mysql-bin.log

#binlog_do_db   = include_database_name

bind-address   = 127.0.0.1

The first of those lines is to uniquely identify our particular server, in our replication configuration. We need to uncomment that line, by removing the "#" before it. The second line indicates the file in which changes to any mysql database or table will be logged.

The third line indicates which databases we want to replicate between our servers. You can add as many databases to this line as you'd like. This article will use a single database named "example" for the purposes of simplicity. And the last line tells our server to accept connections from the internet (by not listening on 127.0.0.1).

server-id   = 1

log_bin   = /var/log/mysql/mysql-bin.log

binlog_do_db   = example

bind-address   = 127.0.0.1

Now we need to restart MySQL:

sudo service mysql restart

We next need to change some command-line settings within our mysql instance. Back at the shell, we can get to our root MySQL user by typing the following:

mysql -u root -p

Please note that the password this command will prompt you for is that of the root MySQL user, not the root user on our server. To confirm that you are logged in to the MySQL shell, the prompt should look like the following.

mysql>

Once we are logged in, we need to run a few commands.

We need to create a pseudo-user that will be used for replicating data between our two VPS. The examples in this article will assume that you name this user "replicator". Replace "password" with the password you wish to use for replication.

create user 'replicator'@'%' identified by 'password';

Now, we have to give this user permission to replicate our MySQL data:

grant replication slave on *.* to 'replicator'@'%';

Permissions for replication cannot, unfortunately, be given on a per-database basis. Our user will only replicate the database(s) that we instruct it to in our configuration file.

For the final step of the initial Server A configuration, we need to get some information about the current MySQL instance which we will later provide to Server B.

The following command will output a few pieces of important information, which we will need to make note of:

show master status;

The output will be looking similar to the following, and will have two pieces of critical information:

```
+------------------+----------+--------------+------------------+
```

```
| File           | Position | Binlog_Do_DB | Binlog_Ignore_DB |

+------------------+----------+--------------+------------------+

| mysql-bin.000001 |    107   | example      |                  |

+------------------+----------+--------------+------------------+
```

1 row in set (0.00 sec)

We need to make a note of the file and position which will be used in the next step.

Step 2 - Install and Configure MySQL on Server B

We need to repeat the same steps that we followed on Server A. First we need to install it, which we can do with the following command:

sudo apt-get install mysql-server mysql-client

Once the two packages are properly installed, we need to configure it in much the same way as we configured Server A. We will start by editing the /etc/mysql/my.cnf file.

sudo nano /etc/mysql/my.cnf

We need to change the same four lines in the configuration file as we changed earlier.

The defaults are listed below, followed by the changes we need to make.

#server-id   = 1

#log_bin   = /var/log/mysql/mysql-bin.log

#binlog_do_db   = include_database_name

bind-address   = 127.0.0.1

We need to change these four lines to match the lines below. Please note, that unlike Server A, the server-id for Server B cannot be set to 1 we already used that ID.

server-id   = 2

log_bin   = /var/log/mysql/mysql-bin.log

binlog_do_db   = example

bind-address   = 127.0.0.1

After you save and quit that file, you need to restart MySQL:

sudo service mysql restart

It is time to go into the MySQL shell and set some more configuration options.

```
mysql -u root -p
```

First, just as on Server A, we are going to create the pseudo-user which will be responsible for the replication. Replace "password" with the password you wish to use.

```
create user 'replicator'@'%' identified by 'password';
```

Next, we need to create the database that we are going to replicate across our VPS.

```
create database example;
```

And we need to give our newly created 'replication' user permissions to replicate it.

```
grant replication slave on *.* to 'replicator'@'%';
```

The next step involves taking the information that we took a note of earlier and applying it to our mysql instance. This will allow replication to begin. The following should be typed at the mysql shell:

```
slave stop;
```

```
CHANGE MASTER TO MASTER_HOST = '3.3.3.3', MASTER_USER =
'replicator', MASTER_PASSWORD = 'password', MASTER_LOG_FILE =
'mysql-bin.000001', MASTER_LOG_POS = 107;
```

```
slave start;
```

You need to replace 'password' with the password that you have chosen for replication. Your values for MASTER_LOG_FILE and MASTER_LOG_POS may differ than those above. You should copy the values that "SHOW MASTER STATUS" returns on Server A.

The last thing we have to do before we complete the MySQL master-master replication is to make note of the master log file and position to use to replicate in the other direction (from Server B to Server A).

We can do that by typing the following:

```
SHOW MASTER STATUS;
```

The output will look similar to the following:

```
+------------------+----------+--------------+------------------+
| File             | Position | Binlog_Do_DB | Binlog_Ignore_DB |
+------------------+----------+--------------+------------------+
| mysql-bin.000004 |    107   | example      |                  |
+------------------+----------+--------------+------------------+
```

1 row in set (0.00 sec)

Take note of the file and position, as we will have to enter those on Server A, to complete the two-way replication.

The next step will explain how to do that.

Step 3 - Completing Replication on Server A

Back on Server A, we need to finish configuring replication on the command line. Running this command will replicate all data from Server B.

slave stop;

CHANGE MASTER TO MASTER_HOST = '4.4.4.4', MASTER_USER = 'replicator', MASTER_PASSWORD = 'password', MASTER_LOG_FILE = 'mysql-bin.000004', MASTER_LOG_POS = 107;

slave start;

Keep in mind that your values may differ from those above. Please also replace the value of MASTER_PASSWORD with the password you created when setting up the replication user.

The output will look similar to the following:

Query OK, 0 rows affected (0.01 sec)

The last thing to do is to test that replication is working on both VPS. The last step will explain an easy way to test this configuration.

And now It should be working, continue on to do some testing.

Step 4 - Testing Master-Master Replication

Now that have all the configuration set up, we are going to test it now. To do this, we are going to create a table in our example database on Server A and check on Server B to see if it shows up. Then, we are going to delete it from Server B and make sure it's no longer showing up on Server A.

We now need to create the database that will be replicated between the servers. We can do that by typing the following at the mysql shell:

create database example;

Once that's done, let's create a dummy table on Server A:

create table example.dummy (`id` varchar(10));

We now are going to check Server B to see if our table exists.

show tables in example;

We should see output similar to the following:

+-------------------+

| Tables_in_example |

+-------------------+

| dummy |

+-------------------+

1 row in set (0.00 sec)

The last test to do is to delete our dummy table from Server B. It should also be deleted from Server A.

We can do this by entering the following on Server B:

DROP TABLE dummy;

To confirm this, running the "show tables" command on Server A will show no tables:

Empty set (0.00 sec)

And there you have it! Working MySQL master-master replication. You can play ping pong with now or actually use it for the greater good.

And as always If you find yourself wanting consulting or further information, then feel free to email me direct at :AsteriskHA@3states.net any time and I will do my best to answer your questions ASAP.

.

Tables

No Database would work without tables and data.

Now we will setup the tables that we are going to need to build our Asterisk system and will set the default values as needed for our system. This won't be hard so don't worry just sit back grab a coffee and continue on.

The next several pages we will setup our database to be useful for our system and you will be getting to know (If you don't already) a little bit about MySql.

Create Database Tables

First we'll login to the MySQL server from the command line with the following command:

mysql -u root -p

In this case, I've specified the user root with the -u flag, and then used the -p flag so MySQL prompts for a password. Enter your current password to complete the login.

you should now be at a MySQL prompt that looks very similar to this:

mysql>

To create a database with the name asterisk type the following command:

CREATE DATABASE asterisk;

then type;

USE asterisk;

now you're ready to create your tables

Then follow the other steps to create the tables needed to run Realtime and for our front ends that we create;

Create table cdr

CDR stands for Call Detail Record, this will create a record for every single call made or received from our system and be very useful for billing as well as basic trouble shooting.

CREATE TABLE `cdr` (

`calldate` **DATETIME NOT NULL DEFAULT** '0000-00-00 00:00:00',

`clid` **VARCHAR**(80) **NOT NULL DEFAULT** '',

`src` **VARCHAR**(80) **NOT NULL DEFAULT** '',

`dst` **VARCHAR**(80) **NOT NULL DEFAULT** '',

`dcontext` **VARCHAR**(80) **NOT NULL DEFAULT** '',

`channel` **VARCHAR**(80) **NOT NULL DEFAULT** '',

`dstchannel` **VARCHAR**(80) **NOT NULL DEFAULT** '',

`lastapp` **VARCHAR**(80) **NOT NULL DEFAULT** '',

`lastdata` **VARCHAR**(80) **NOT NULL DEFAULT** '',

`duration` **INT**(11) **NOT NULL DEFAULT** '0',

`billsec` **INT**(11) **NOT NULL DEFAULT** '0',

`disposition` **VARCHAR**(45) **NOT NULL DEFAULT** '',

`amaflags` **INT**(11) **NOT NULL DEFAULT** '0',

`accountcode` **VARCHAR**(20) **NOT NULL DEFAULT** '',

`userfield` **VARCHAR**(255) **NOT NULL DEFAULT** '',

`uniqueid` **VARCHAR**(32) **NOT NULL DEFAULT** '',

`linkedid` **VARCHAR**(32) **NOT NULL DEFAULT** '',

`sequence` **VARCHAR**(32) **NOT NULL DEFAULT** '',

```
`peeraccount` VARCHAR(32) NOT NULL DEFAULT '',

INDEX `calldate` (`calldate`),

INDEX `dst` (`dst`),

INDEX `accountcode` (`accountcode`)

)

COLLATE='latin1_swedish_ci'

ENGINE=InnoDB;
```

Create table extensions

The Extension table purpose is to tell each and every call made or received where to go and how to get there. We can also setup, change and manipulate many different variables from here as well.

```
CREATE TABLE `extensions` (

`id` INT(11) NOT NULL AUTO_INCREMENT,

`context` VARCHAR(20) NOT NULL DEFAULT '',

`exten` VARCHAR(20) NOT NULL DEFAULT '',

`priority` TINYINT(4) NOT NULL DEFAULT '0',

`app` VARCHAR(20) NOT NULL DEFAULT '',

`appdata` VARCHAR(128) NOT NULL DEFAULT '',

PRIMARY KEY (`context`, `exten`, `priority`),

INDEX `id` (`id`)

)

COLLATE='latin1_swedish_ci'

ENGINE=MyISAM

AUTO_INCREMENT=290;
```

Create table meetme

We've all have had a conference call at one time or another and this is the table that provides the information to asterisk so we can provide our own conference bridges.

```
CREATE TABLE `meetme` (
`confno` VARCHAR(80) NOT NULL DEFAULT '0',
`username` VARCHAR(64) NOT NULL DEFAULT '',
`domain` VARCHAR(128) NOT NULL DEFAULT '',
`pin` VARCHAR(20) NULL DEFAULT NULL,
`adminpin` VARCHAR(20) NULL DEFAULT NULL,
`members` INT(11) NOT NULL DEFAULT '0',
PRIMARY KEY (`confno`)
)
COLLATE='latin1_swedish_ci'
ENGINE=MyISAM;
```

Create table queue_table

This table is used to create call queues, that's where you have agents logged into the queue and as they agent becomes available the call is transferred to them.

CREATE TABLE `queue_table` (

`name` **VARCHAR**(128) **NOT NULL,**

`musiconhold` **VARCHAR**(128) **NULL DEFAULT NULL,**

`announce` **VARCHAR**(128) **NULL DEFAULT NULL,**

`context` **VARCHAR**(128) **NULL DEFAULT NULL,**

`timeout` **INT**(11) **NULL DEFAULT NULL,**

`monitor_join` **TINYINT**(1) **NULL DEFAULT NULL,**

`monitor_format` **VARCHAR**(128) **NULL DEFAULT NULL,**

`queue_youarenext` **VARCHAR**(128) **NULL DEFAULT NULL,**

`queue_thereare` **VARCHAR**(128) **NULL DEFAULT NULL,**

`queue_callswaiting` **VARCHAR**(128) **NULL DEFAULT NULL,**

`queue_holdtime` **VARCHAR**(128) **NULL DEFAULT NULL,**

`queue_minutes` **VARCHAR**(128) **NULL DEFAULT NULL,**

`queue_seconds` **VARCHAR**(128) **NULL DEFAULT NULL,**

`queue_lessthan` **VARCHAR**(128) **NULL DEFAULT NULL,**

`queue_thankyou` **VARCHAR**(128) **NULL DEFAULT NULL,**

`queue_reporthold` **VARCHAR**(128) **NULL DEFAULT NULL,**

`announce_frequency` **INT**(11) **NULL DEFAULT NULL,**

`announce_round_seconds` **INT**(11) **NULL DEFAULT NULL,**

```sql
`announce_holdtime` VARCHAR(128) NULL DEFAULT NULL,

`retry` INT(11) NULL DEFAULT NULL,

`wrapuptime` INT(11) NULL DEFAULT NULL,

`maxlen` INT(11) NULL DEFAULT NULL,

`servicelevel` INT(11) NULL DEFAULT NULL,

`strategy` VARCHAR(128) NULL DEFAULT NULL,

`joinempty` VARCHAR(128) NULL DEFAULT NULL,

`leavewhenempty` VARCHAR(128) NULL DEFAULT NULL,

`eventmemberstatus` TINYINT(1) NULL DEFAULT NULL,

`eventwhencalled` TINYINT(1) NULL DEFAULT NULL,

`reportholdtime` TINYINT(1) NULL DEFAULT NULL,

`memberdelay` INT(11) NULL DEFAULT NULL,

`weight` INT(11) NULL DEFAULT NULL,

`timeoutrestart` TINYINT(1) NULL DEFAULT NULL,

`periodic_announce` VARCHAR(50) NULL DEFAULT NULL,

`periodic_announce_frequency` INT(11) NULL DEFAULT NULL,

`ringinuse` TINYINT(1) NULL DEFAULT NULL,

`setinterfacevar` TINYINT(1) NULL DEFAULT NULL,

PRIMARY KEY (`name`)

)

COLLATE='latin1_swedish_ci'

ENGINE=MyISAM;
```

Create table queue_member_table

This tables says who is a member to what queue.

```sql
CREATE TABLE `queue_member_table` (
`uniqueid` INT(10) UNSIGNED NOT NULL AUTO_INCREMENT,
`membername` VARCHAR(40) NULL DEFAULT NULL,
`queue_name` VARCHAR(128) NULL DEFAULT NULL,
`interface` VARCHAR(128) NULL DEFAULT NULL,
`penalty` INT(11) NULL DEFAULT NULL,
`paused` INT(11) NULL DEFAULT NULL,
PRIMARY KEY (`uniqueid`),
UNIQUE INDEX `queue_interface` (`queue_name`, `interface`)
)
COLLATE='latin1_swedish_ci'
ENGINE=MyISAM
AUTO_INCREMENT=6;
```

Create table sip_buddies

This table is the one that identifies the devices on the asterisk system as well as all the useful information to make quality calls.

CREATE TABLE `sip_buddies` (

`id` **INT**(11) **NOT NULL AUTO_INCREMENT**,

`name` **VARCHAR**(80) **NOT NULL**,

`callerid` **VARCHAR**(80) **NULL DEFAULT NULL**,

`defaultuser` **VARCHAR**(80) **NOT NULL**,

`regexten` **VARCHAR**(80) **NOT NULL**,

`secret` **VARCHAR**(80) **NULL DEFAULT** 'Sardis43946',

`mailbox` **VARCHAR**(50) **NULL DEFAULT NULL**,

`accountcode` **VARCHAR**(20) **NULL DEFAULT NULL**,

`callbackextension` **VARCHAR**(20) **NULL DEFAULT NULL**,

`context` **VARCHAR**(80) **NULL DEFAULT** 'standard-customer',

`amaflags` **VARCHAR**(7) **NULL DEFAULT NULL**,

`callgroup` **VARCHAR**(10) **NULL DEFAULT NULL**,

`canreinvite` **CHAR**(3) **NULL DEFAULT** 'no',

`defaultip` **VARCHAR**(15) **NULL DEFAULT NULL**,

`dtmfmode` **VARCHAR**(7) **NULL DEFAULT NULL**,

`fromuser` **VARCHAR**(80) **NULL DEFAULT NULL**,

`fromdomain` **VARCHAR**(80) **NULL DEFAULT NULL**,

`fullcontact` **VARCHAR**(80) **NULL DEFAULT NULL**,

`host` **VARCHAR**(31) **NOT NULL DEFAULT** 'dynamic',

```
`insecure` VARCHAR(4) NULL DEFAULT NULL,

`language` CHAR(2) NULL DEFAULT NULL,

`md5secret` VARCHAR(80) NULL DEFAULT NULL,

`nat` VARCHAR(15) NOT NULL DEFAULT 'no',

`deny` VARCHAR(95) NULL DEFAULT NULL,

`permit` VARCHAR(95) NULL DEFAULT NULL,

`mask` VARCHAR(95) NULL DEFAULT NULL,

`pickupgroup` VARCHAR(10) NULL DEFAULT NULL,

`port` VARCHAR(5) NOT NULL,

`qualify` CHAR(4) NULL DEFAULT 'yes',

`restrictcid` CHAR(1) NULL DEFAULT NULL,

`rtptimeout` CHAR(3) NULL DEFAULT NULL,

`rtpholdtimeout` CHAR(3) NULL DEFAULT NULL,

`type` VARCHAR(6) NOT NULL DEFAULT 'friend',

`disallow` VARCHAR(100) NULL DEFAULT 'all',

`allow` VARCHAR(100) NULL DEFAULT 'g729;ilbc;gsm;ulaw;alaw',

`musiconhold` VARCHAR(100) NULL DEFAULT NULL,

`regseconds` INT(11) NOT NULL DEFAULT '0',

`ipaddr` VARCHAR(15) NOT NULL,

`cancallforward` CHAR(3) NULL DEFAULT 'yes',

`lastms` INT(11) NOT NULL,

`useragent` CHAR(255) NULL DEFAULT NULL,

`regserver` VARCHAR(100) NULL DEFAULT NULL,

`Description` VARCHAR(100) NULL DEFAULT NULL,
```

```
PRIMARY KEY (`id`),

UNIQUE INDEX `name` (`name`),

INDEX `name_2` (`name`)

)

COMMENT='callbackextension'

COLLATE='latin1_swedish_ci'

ENGINE=MyISAM

AUTO_INCREMENT=972;
```

Create table voicemail_users

Well if you want voicemail then you have to be in this table or asterisk won't recognize that you have the permissions to have voicemail.

```
CREATE TABLE `voicemail_users` (
`uniqueid` INT(11) NOT NULL AUTO_INCREMENT,
`customer_id` VARCHAR(11) NOT NULL DEFAULT '0',
`context` VARCHAR(50) NOT NULL,
`mailbox` VARCHAR(11) NOT NULL DEFAULT '0',
`password` VARCHAR(5) NOT NULL DEFAULT '0',
`fullname` VARCHAR(150) NOT NULL,
`email` VARCHAR(50) NOT NULL,
`pager` VARCHAR(50) NOT NULL,
`tz` VARCHAR(10) NOT NULL DEFAULT 'eastern',
`attach` VARCHAR(4) NOT NULL DEFAULT 'yes',
`saycid` VARCHAR(4) NOT NULL DEFAULT 'yes',
`dialout` VARCHAR(10) NOT NULL,
`callback` VARCHAR(10) NOT NULL,
`review` VARCHAR(4) NOT NULL DEFAULT 'no',
`operator` VARCHAR(4) NOT NULL DEFAULT 'no',
`envelope` VARCHAR(4) NOT NULL DEFAULT 'no',
`sayduration` VARCHAR(4) NOT NULL DEFAULT 'no',
`saydurationm` TINYINT(4) NOT NULL DEFAULT '1',
`sendvoicemail` VARCHAR(4) NOT NULL DEFAULT 'no',
```

```sql
`delete` VARCHAR(4) NOT NULL DEFAULT 'no',

`nextaftercmd` VARCHAR(4) NOT NULL DEFAULT 'yes',

`forcename` VARCHAR(4) NOT NULL DEFAULT 'no',

`forcegreetings` VARCHAR(4) NOT NULL DEFAULT 'no',

`hidefromdir` VARCHAR(4) NOT NULL DEFAULT 'yes',

`stamp` TIMESTAMP NOT NULL DEFAULT CURRENT_TIMESTAMP ON UPDATE CURRENT_TIMESTAMP,

PRIMARY KEY (`uniqueid`),

INDEX `mailbox_context` (`mailbox`, `context`)

)

COLLATE='latin1_swedish_ci'

ENGINE=MyISAM

AUTO_INCREMENT=2010;
```

Now What

Pat yourself on the back you now have a real Database server installed that has full redundancy. It may very well be the first time ever you have been in front of so much power, we've all heard that knowledge is power and we all know that knowledge is data.

With this knowledge we can not only use it to manipulate asterisk but permit our frontends to easily troubleshoot, create users, delete users, bill users and a lot more that you will learn in the other book Building an Asterisk GUI in C#: Proven Method http://amzn.to/1negZhM and you can feel free to get on the mailing list for it here by Request notification of new releases send an email to TechBook-mailinglist@3states.net.

If you find yourself wanting consulting or further information, then feel free to email me direct at My Direct Email AsteriskHA@3states.net any time and I will do my best to answer your questions ASAP

Asterisk

Now the fun begins, or at least I think so. Let's learn a little about asterisk really quick so that you may get as excited about it as I am. Remember you are limited only by your ability to think of new possibilities because it's all here at your fingertips and most of the current features were added by either request or an individual creating a feature and publishing it.

So here is the canned version of what asterisk is and what it can do;

Asterisk is a software implementation of a telephone private branch exchange (PBX); it allows attached telephones to make calls to one another, and to connect to other telephone services, such as the public switched telephone network (PSTN) and Voice over Internet Protocol (VoIP) services. Its name comes from the asterisk symbol, *.

Asterisk is released with a dual license model, using the GNU General Public License (GPL) as a free software license and a proprietary software license to permit licensees to distribute proprietary, unpublished system components.

Asterisk was created in 1999 by Mark Spencer of Digium. Originally designed for Linux, Asterisk runs on a variety of operating systems, including NetBSD, OpenBSD, FreeBSD, Mac OS X, and Solaris. Asterisk is small enough to run in an embedded environment such as Customer-premises equipment-hardware running OpenWrt, there are complete self-contained versions that can boot from a storage device such as a flash drive or external disk drive (preferably IDE/PATA, SATA or mSATA; a USB-connected device can be used, but is often not recommended). A live CD or virtual machine can also be used.

The Asterisk software includes many features available in proprietary PBX systems: voice mail, conference calling, interactive voice response (phone menus), and automatic call distribution. Users can create new functionality by writing dial plan scripts in several of Asterisk's own *extensions* languages, by adding custom loadable modules written in C, or by implementing *Asterisk Gateway Interface* (AGI) programs using any programming language capable of communicating via the standard streams system (stdin and stdout) or by network TCP sockets.

Asterisk supports several standard voice over IP protocols, including the Session Initiation Protocol (SIP), the Media Gateway Control Protocol (MGCP), and H.323. Asterisk supports most SIP telephones, acting both as registrar and back-to-back user agent, and can serve as a gateway between IP phones and the public switched telephone network (PSTN) via T- or E-carrier interfaces or analog FXO cards. The Inter-Asterisk eXchange (IAX) protocol, RFC 5456, native to Asterisk, provides efficient trunking of calls among Asterisk PBXes, in addition to distributing some configuration logic. Many VoIP service providers support it for call completion into the PSTN, often because they themselves have deployed Asterisk or offer it as a hosted application. Some telephones also support the IAX protocol.

By supporting a variety of traditional and VoIP telephony services, Asterisk allows to build telephone systems, or migrate existing systems to deploy new technologies. Some sites are using Asterisk to replace proprietary PBXes, others provide additional features, such as voice mail or voice response menus, or virtual call shops, or to reduce cost by carrying long-distance calls over the Internet (toll bypass).

In addition to VoIP protocols, Asterisk supports traditional circuit-switching protocols such as ISDN and SS7. This requires appropriate hardware interface cards, marketed by third-party vendors. Each protocol requires the installation of software modules.

Asterisk-based telephony solutions offer a rich and flexible feature set. Asterisk offers both classical PBX functionality and advanced features, and interoperates with traditional standards-based telephony systems and Voice over IP systems. Asterisk offers the advanced features that are often associated with large, high end (and high cost) proprietary PBXs. The list below includes a sample of the features available in Asterisk.

Features

While extensive, I felt it to be unjust not to list the many features that Asterisk has readily available. This section can be skipped however I do not recommend skipping it as in doing so will hurt your understanding of the many different possibilities that are at your fingertips.

I will not go into great details in listing them, however I may put some explanations on the more relevant features. For complete details feel free to do a google search or wait until my next book Building an Asterisk GUI in C#: Proven Method http://amzn.to/1negZhM and you can feel free to get on the mailing list for it here by Request notification of new releases send an email to TechBook-mailinglist@3states.net .

So read on and enjoy the empowerment that awaits you.

Call Features

ADSI On-Screen Menu System
Alarm Receiver
Append Message
Authentication
Automated Attendant
Blacklists
Blind Transfer
Call Detail Records
Call Forward on Busy
Call Forward on No Answer
Call Forward Variable
Call Monitoring
Call Parking
Call Queuing
Call Recording
Call Retrieval
Call Routing (DID & ANI)
Call Snooping
Call Transfer
Call Waiting
Caller ID
Caller ID Blocking
Caller ID on Call Waiting
Calling Cards
Conference Bridging
Database Store / Retrieve
Database Integration
Dial by Name
Direct Inward System Access
Distinctive Ring
Distributed Universal Number Discovery (DUNDi™)
Do Not Disturb
E911
ENUM
Fax Transmit and Receive
Flexible Extension Logic
Interactive Directory Listing

Interactive Voice Response (IVR)
Local and Remote Call Agents
Macros
Music On Hold
Music On Transfer:

Flexible Mp3-based System

Random or Linear Play

Volume Control

Privacy

Open Settlement Protocol (OSP)
Overhead Paging
Protocol Conversion
Remote Call Pickup
Remote Office Support
Roaming Extensions
Route by Caller ID
SMS Messaging
Spell / Say
Streaming Hold Music
Supervised Transfer
Talk Detection
Text-to-Speech (via Festival)
Three-way Calling
Time and Date
Transcoding
Trunking
VoIP Gateways
Voicemail:

Visual Indicator for Message Waiting

Stutter Dial tone for Message Waiting

Voicemail to email

Voicemail Groups

Web Voicemail Interface

Zapateller – have Asterisk in a lot of cases eliminate telemarketing calls.

We all hate telemarketers and this handy little tool will help you deal with them. A must have for offices and people who like privacy.

Computer-Telephony Integration

Asterisk Gateway Interface (AGI)
Asterisk Manager Interface (AMI)
Asterisk REST Interface (ARI)
Outbound Call Spooling

Scalability

TDMoE (Time Division Multiplex over Ethernet)
Allows direct connection of Asterisk PBX
Zero latency
Uses commodity Ethernet hardware
Voice-over IP
Allows for integration of physically separate installations
Uses commonly deployed data connections
Allows a unified dial plan across multiple offices

With the many different options available and a mind that can think outside of the box then scalability is really only limited by your own mind. I have implemented systems with well over 2500 users, systems that are back-ends to CRMs, systems that are back-ends for many other programs and systems that are used for emergency communications.

So dream and you can make Asterisk do what you can dream of.

Speech

Cepstral TTS
Lumenvox ASR

Speech has become a feature that is more and more desired for things like reading emails to instructions as well as providing the end user with useful information for whatever reason one can think of. The thing about speech is in the beginning it was all very computerized in the sound and anyone could pick out a computer generated voice. With the new technologies out there, speech is becoming more and more human like and being used more and more as it progresses.

There are lots of speech technologies out there that are both free as well as paid versions. Play with them and think of some new implementations that no one else has come up with.

Codecs

ADPCM
CELT (pass through)
G.711 (A-Law & μ-Law)
G.719 (pass through)
G.722
G.722.1 licensed from Polycom®
G.722.1 Annex C licensed from Polycom®
G.723.1 (pass through)
G.726
G.729a
GSM
iLBC
Linear
LPC-10
Speex
SILK

Codecs is where a lot of the magic is done and instead of trying to explain we will give the internet's explanation.

A **codec** is a device or computer program capable of encoding or decoding a digital data stream or signal

A codec encodes a data stream or signal for transmission, storage or encryption, or decodes it for playback or editing. Codecs are used in videoconferencing, streaming media and video editing applications. A video camera's analog-to-digital converter (ADC) converts its analog signals into digital signals, which are then passed through a video compressor for digital transmission or storage. A receiving device then runs the signal through a video decompressor, then a digital-to-analog converter (DAC) for analog display.

VoIP Protocols

Google Talk
H.323
IAX™ (Inter-Asterisk eXchange)
Jingle/XMPP
MGCP (Media Gateway Control Protocol
SCCP (Cisco® Skinny®)
SIP (Session Initiation Protocol)
UNIStim

Traditional Telephony Protocols

E&M
E&M Wink
Feature Group D
FXS
FXO
GR-303
Loopstart
Groundstart
Kewlstart
MF and DTMF support
Robbed-bit Signaling (RBS) Types

Protocols are used to send critical information in with different standards and compressions ratios. They make everything sound good or bad depending on what one and what compression you are using.

ISDN Protocols

AT&T 4ESS
EuroISDN PRI and BRI
Lucent 5ESS
National ISDN 1
National ISDN 2
NFAS
Nortel DMS100
Q.SIG

Installing

Asterisk at first glance looks like any idiot can install and use it. They have "Live CD's", "RPM packages" and a ton of GUI's that work for those that don't want or need carrier class service. Skip past those because they will NOT be what I recommend and while they are marked as stable they are NOT what a serious carrier would ever think of using. Find the source code for asterisks here is the links as of when this book was written along with download instructions.

While I still use wget and just copy the download links to the wget command, the official instructions use git.

#cd /usr/src

git clone http://gerrit.asterisk.org/asterisk asterisk

git clone git://git.asterisk.org/dahdi/linux dahdi-linux

git clone git://git.asterisk.org/dahdi/tools dahdi-tools

svn checkout http://svn.asterisk.org/svn/libpri/branches/1.4 libpri

Ok now you've got the source code and need to do something with it.

Installation instructions;

Run the following commands and un-compress those weird looking files. Keep in mind to make the file name adjustments so that they match what you have in the directory, if you don't know what you have then type "ls" and that will list the current contents of the directory you're in.

tar -zxvf libpri-1.X.Y.tar.gz

```
# tar -zxvf dahdi-linux-complete-2.X.Y+2.X.Y.tar.gz
```

```
# tar -zxvf asterisk-11-current.tar.gz
```

Now when you run an "ls" you will notice that there are 3 new folders named just like the files but without the "tar.gz" on the end. We can now start building. Follow in the order given below.

DAHDI

```
# cd dahdi-linux-complete-2.X.Y+2.X.Y
```

```
# make
```

```
# make install
```

```
# make config
```

LibPri - this is only needed if you are going to be using PRI's for connectivity instead of VOIP

```
# cd ../libpri-1.X.Y
```
```
# make
```

```
# make install
```

PJProject.

Make sure all supporting libraries are installed.

cd / /usr/src/asterisk-11.20.0/contrib/scripts

./install_prereq

There was a time where you had to spend hours to make sure your system had all of the desired and required libraries installed and in their correct places. There is still some software out there that if you use the source code to install will throw errors left and right as you go through and learn what all the dependencies are and install them one at a time.

So this tool is useful and I recommend that you use it every time you do an install or upgrade.

Special Configuration

The only things that is needed here that is not listed in other areas of this guide are listed below and as you can see there are very little changes that need to be made. It is important to note that your configuration will differ from mine. There are unlimited possibilities here and your creativity is the length of the possibilities that you are restricted to.

cdr_mysql.conf

```
[global]

hostname=(The IP of this machine)

dbname=asterisk

table=cdr

password=(Password for MySql)

user=(Username for MySql)

port=3306
```

extconfig.conf

These are the tables that we created earlier, remember?

[settings]

sippeers => mysql,general,sip_buddies

sipusers => mysql,general,sip_buddies

extensions => mysql,general,extensions

voicemail => mysql,general,voicemail_users

queues => mysql,general,queue_table

queue_members => mysql,general,queue_member_table

meetme => mysql,general,meetme

extensions.conf

The important thing in this file is to locate the context that we will have tables for in the database and place in it "switch => Realtime" as we did bwlow;

[general]

static=yes

writeprotect=no

clearglobalvars=no

[globals]

CONSOLE=Console/dsp

 [local]

switch => Realtime

 ignorepat => 9

include => default

include => parkedcalls

[from-sip-external1]

switch => Realtime

[default]

switch => Realtime

 [standard-customer]

switch => Realtime

[out-bound]

[GetNumber]

switch => Realtime

modules.conf

```
[modules]
autoload=yes
noload => pbx_gtkconsole.so
noload => codec_dahdi.so
noload => chan_motif.so
noload => cel_pgsql.so
noload => cel_tds.so
noload => res_config_ldap.so
noload => res_config_pgsql.so
noload => res_corosync.so
load => res_musiconhold.so
noload => chan_alsa.so
noload => chan_console.so
;
```

res_config_mysql.conf

```
[general]

dbhost = (The IP of this machine)

dbname = asterisk

dbuser = (Username for MySql)

dbpass = (Password for MySql)

dbport = 3306

dbcharset = latin1
```

sip.Conf

```
[general]

context=public          ; Default context for incoming calls. Defaults to 'default'

allowoverlap=no          ; Disable overlap dialing support. (Default is yes)

udpbindaddr= (Put your IP Here) ; IP address to bind UDP listen socket to (0.0.0.0
binds to all)

tcpenable=no          ; Enable server for incoming TCP connections (default is
no)

tcpbindaddr=0.0.0.0          ; IP address for TCP server to bind to (0.0.0.0 binds to
all interfaces)

transport=udp          ; Set the default transports.  The order determines the
primary default transport.

srvlookup=no          ; Enable DNS SRV lookups on outbound calls

rtcachefriends=yes          ; Cache realtime friends by adding them to the internal
list

rtsavesysname=yes          ; Save systemname in realtime database at
registration

rtupdate=yes          ; Send registry updates to database using realtime?
(yes|no)

tautoclear=yes          ; Auto-Expire friends created on the fly on the same
schedule

[authentication]

[basic-options](!)          ; a template

    dtmfmode=rfc2833

    context=from-office

    type=friend

[natted-phone](!,basic-options)   ; another template inheriting basic-options

    directmedia=no
```

74

```
    host=dynamic

[public-phone](!,basic-options)   ; another template inheriting basic-options

    directmedia=yes

[my-codecs](!)              ; a template for my preferred codecs

    disallow=all

    allow=g711

    allow=gsm

    allow=ulaw

    allow=alaw
```

RealTime

RealTime lets Asterisk run configurations from the MySql database mostly anyways and this makes a HA option readily available due to the nature of the MySql database setup that we've done.

From voip-info here is realtime explanation;

"The Asterisk external configuration engine is the result of work by Anthony Minessale II, Mark Spencer and Constantine Filin It is designed to provide a flexible, seamless integration between Asterisk's internal configuration structure and external SQL other databases (maybe even LDAP one day).

External configuration is configured in /etc/asterisk/extconfig.conf allowing you to map any configuration file (static mappings) to be pulled from the database, or to map special runtime entries which permit the dynamic creation of objects, entities, peers, etc. without the necessity of a reload."

Olle explains the world

In the new RealTime architecture, all database specific code is moved to database specific drivers. The channel just calls a generic routine to do database lookup. Much cleaner, simpler and manageable from a coding standpoint.

You can read a lot more about it in my new book Building an Asterisk GUI in C#: Proven Method at http://amzn.to/1negZhM and you can feel free to get on the mailing list for it here by Request notification of new releases at TechBook-mailinglist@3states.net.

Three ways to access the data

STATIC: This is used to load static configuration when a module is loaded

REALTIME: This is used to lookup objects during a call (or another event)

UPDATE: This is used to update objects

The database support in the channel is not changed. There are "normal" static peers/users and database peers/users. The **static ones**, regardless if these are loaded from a text file or a database configuration, are kept in-memory and in the SIP channel we provide them with NAT traversal support and message waiting indication if needed.

The **database peers/users** are not kept in memory. These are only loaded when we have a call and then deleted, so **there's no support for NAT keep-alives (qualify=) or voicemail indications** for these peers.
NOTE: If you enable RealTime caching in your sip.conf, Voicemail MWI works and so does 'sip show peers' - see rtcachefriends=yes. The downside to this is that if you change anything in the database, you need to do a 'sip reload' (for major changes) or 'sip prune realtime PEERNAME' (for single peer changes) before they become active.

In laymen's terms

In the Stable 1.0.X branch of Asterisk, database storage of configuration files and parameters was done mostly by hardcoding connection and query code directly into the application. The best example of this is in app_voicemail, where you can see MySQL code and PostgreSQL code all meshed with the app_voicemail code.

This method of database retrieval proves to be ugly as all the asterisk code is now crammed with database specific code that is irrelevant to the function of the application at hand. But RealTime was developed as a means to remove the code and replace it with a unified (abstracted) database retrieval method."

While we can make several hundred possible combinations for configurations, I will let you decide what you want and I will post Voip-Info's setup information here as a reference.

Terminology/Files

Driver - A compiled module containing database specific code that accepts the generalized function calls that RealTime makes. As of this writing, only ODBC, MySQL (via asterisk-addons) and LDAP (see http://free.oxymium.net/Asterisk/ and http://bugs.digium.com/view.php?id=5768) drivers are available.

Family - A name associated with a RealTime call. Examples: sippeers, sipusers, voicemail.

extconfig.conf - The configuration file that contains the information necessary to bind specific families to specific drivers.

res_odbc.conf - The configuration file for ODBC RealTime.

res_mysql.conf - The configuration file for MySQL RealTime.

res_ldap.conf - The configuration file for LDAP RealTime.

ODBC - Open DataBase Connectivity

MySQL - the world's most popular open source database

OpenLDAP - Open source implementation of the Lightweight Directory Access Protocol

There are 2 methods of using RealTime: ODBC and MySQL. Yes, you can use ODBC to connect to MySQL and many other ODBC supported databases. (Being an avid MySQL user and advocate, I didn't want to bother with ODBC so I wrote the RealTime MySQL driver over the weekend.)

How to configure RealTime - ODBC Method

This paragraph assumes you have ODBC already running and installed on your box.)

When you start to compile Asterisk, the Makefile inside res/ should detect if you have ODBC properly installed and if so compile the res_config_odbc.so module for you (as long as you have the unixODBC-dev libraries installed - http://sourceforge.net/project/showfiles.php?group_id=1544&package_id=122072.

Go into /etc/asterisk/res_odbc.conf and configure your ODBC connections. Some sample configs are supplied in asterisk/configs/res_odbc.conf.sample **NOTE**: res_config_odbc.conf is deprecated and will not be loaded.

How to configure RealTime - MySQL Method

This page assumes you have the MySQL client libraries/headers installed on your box.)
Check out asterisk-addons from CVS:

cd /usr/src/
svn co http://svn.digium.com/svn/asterisk-addons/trunk asterisk-addons

Go into asterisk-addons and run the following commands

configure
make
make install (This will also compile and install the other stuff in addons so if you don't want/need it, just run 'make' and manually copy res_config_mysql.so to your modules directory.

Copy asterisk-addons/configs/res_mysql.conf.sample to /etc/asterisk/res_mysql.conf
Edit this file to your liking. At this time, the MySQL drivers supports multiple databases on only one server.

Now its time to edit /etc/asterisk/extconfig.conf

Extconfig - Static Configs

Static configuration is where you can store regular *. conf files into the database. These configurations are read at Asterisk startup/reload. Some modules may also re-read this info upon their own reload (Ex. sip reload). Here is the format for a static config:

[settings]

<conf filename> =>
<driver>,<databasename>~np~[~/np~,table_name~np~]~/np~

queues.conf => odbc,asterisk,ast_config

sip.conf => mysql,asterisk

iax.conf => ldap,MyBaseDN,iax

Above we have 3 examples. The first example will bind 'queues.conf' to the table 'ast_config' located in the database context 'asterisk' using the ODBC driver. — **NOTE (LN): this is NOT the database you specified in /etc/odbc.ini, rather it's the context in /etc/asterisk/res_odbc.conf that you are using to connect to the ODBC driver!**
The second example will bind 'sip.conf' to the table 'sip.conf' (because we ommited the table name, it defaults to the file name) in the database 'asterisk' using the MySQL driver.
The 3rd one will bind iax.conf to the 'table' iax.conf in the ldap database using LDAP driver; MyBaseDN is the base DN for the query.
Using the above examples, now, when app_queue.so loads, the RealTime ODBC driver will execute a query and get the information it needs. The same is true for chan_sip.so, but with MySQL and chan_iax.so with LDAP.

Extconfig – RealTime

RealTime configuration is where configuration values are read/updated in real time.

Example: Let's say you have 2 SIP users defined in your sip.conf and you want to add a 3rd. You add them to the file then execute the command 'sip reload'. This re-reads your sip.conf and allows the 3rd to register. With RealTime, all you do is add 1 new record to the table that sipusers has been bound to. No reloading necessary.

RealTime maps take the following format:

[settings]

<family name> => <driver>,<database name>~np~[~/np~,table_name~np~]~/np~

sippeers => mysql,general,sip_buddies

sipusers => mysql,general,sip_buddies

extensions => mysql,general,extensions

voicemail => mysql,general,voicemail_users

queues => mysql,general,queue_table

queue_members => mysql,general,queue_member_table

meetme => mysql,general,meetme

Above we have Seven examples. The first example will bind the family name "sippeers" to the table " sip_buddies " in the database "asterisk" using the MySQL driver.

It is worth noting that sipusers and sippeers may both refer to the same table, if you wish.

NOTE: extconfig.conf is parsed each time you connect to the asterisk CLI.

Now that you have created all the necessary binds, it is time to create the tables. Since the tables are different to each family, I've broken the Wiki pages down to eliminate 1 huge RealTime page. Scroll down to the bottom to find the individual family pages.

NOTE: If you are setting up only IAX users (no peers), both iaxusers and iaxpeers entries in the above file need to be either included (uncommented) for iax users/peers to be loaded from the database.

A follow-up book will discuss development of GUI's that run on separate machines and are very efficient as well as robust. Keep an eye out for them or email AsteriskHA@3states.net me to receive a notification of the release.

A follow-up book will discuss advanced configuration of Asterisk. Keep an eye out for Building an Asterisk GUI in C#: Proven Method at http://amzn.to/1negZhM and you can feel free to get on the mailing list for it here by Request notification of new releases.

In the meantime, congratulate yourself on a job well done and play a little with it and see what the possibilities are as well as coming up with even more ideals on configurations.

And yea I'm just a little shameful in the self-promotion of my new book Building an Asterisk GUI in C#: Proven Method at http://amzn.to/1negZhM and think you should sign up for the mailing list of new releases so go ahead and Request notification of new releases at TechBook-mailinglist@3states.net.

One more note here if you need help then feel free to email me at Asterisk High Availability at AsteriskHA@3states.net.

Interfaces GUI's

Now we get to play and here you can do it from your favorite development platform, I prefer C# so that's what I will use. I see many different systems out there for administrating Asterisk that are written in php and run on the same as Asterisk does, I believe that while you may be able to build such a system and not ever run into an issue with that configuration, I do not endorse those methods. It is possible to run many different roles and configurations on a Linux box and many do but I cation you to be careful and to avoid those low class ghetto scenarios at all cost and I base that on eighteen years' experience in the VoIP world.

A follow-up book will discuss development of GUI's that run on separate machines and are very efficient as well as robust.

Keep an eye out for Building an Asterisk GUI in C#: Proven Method at http://amzn.to/1negZhM and you can feel free to get on the mailing list for it here by Request notification of new releases at TechBook-mailinglist@3states.net.

www.ingramcontent.com/pod-product-compliance
Lightning Source LLC
Chambersburg PA
CBHW061019050326
40689CB00012B/2681